THE BEARS NATURE GUIDE

Almost everything small bears and kids need to know about...

the animals
the plants
the earth itself

with actual facts about frogs, possums, birds, fish, trees, rocks, ladybugs, earthquakes...

and lots more

by Stan and Jan Berenstain

Random House · New York

Manufactured in the United States of America

ISBN: 0-590-75813-6

This edition published by arrangement with Random House. For rights information write: Random House, Inc., 201 E. 50th Street, New York, N.Y. 10022.

Come!
The wonders of nature
await you outside
with me, Papa Bear,
as your nature walk guide.

In all my years
as a nature guide
I have followed one rule
far and wide:

Be alert for any
sign or sound –
the wonders of nature
are all around!

ACTUAL FACTS ABOUT NATURE

WHAT IS NATURE?

It's everybody
and everything—

a peacock's tail,

a butterfly's wing.

It's snails

and stones

and dinosaur bones.

Volcanoes!

Earthquakes . . .

Cousin Liz!

That's just a PART

of what nature is.

Nature is
THE WORLD OF ANIMALS—

from the biggest whale . . .

to the smallest flea.

IT'S THE WORLD OF PLANTS—

from the tiniest weed . . .

to the tallest tree.

IT'S THE EARTH ITSELF —

the rocks . . .
and soil.

And from under the earth

come coal and oil.

ARE YOU AN ANIMAL ?

1. Animals are living things

So whether
you're a bear
or a bird
or a honey bee,

if you're ALIVE,
you just might be—

an ANIMAL.

2. Animals can move around

They can walk or run,

fly or glide,

swim,

jump,

crawl,

or slide.

Plants can't
move around.
They are rooted
to the ground.

So,
if you're ALIVE
and MOVE AROUND
and are not rooted
to the ground,
then it seems,
at least so far,
an animal
is what you are.

ACTUAL
FACTUAL
BEAR

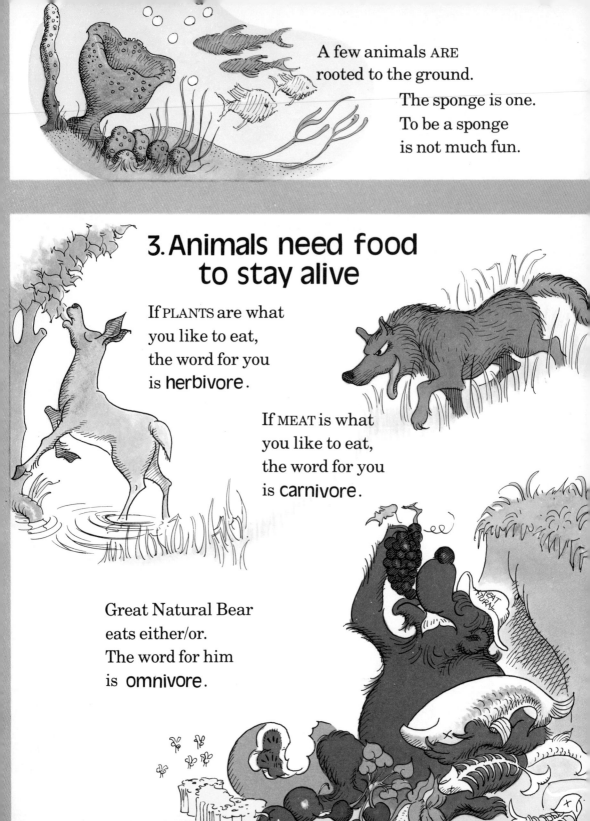

A few animals ARE
rooted to the ground.

The sponge is one.
To be a sponge
is not much fun.

3. Animals need food
to stay alive

If PLANTS are what
you like to eat,
the word for you
is **herbivore**.

If MEAT is what
you like to eat,
the word for you
is **carnivore**.

Great Natural Bear
eats either/or.
The word for him
is **omnivore**.

4. Animals reproduce

A good thing, too!
If they didn't,
there wouldn't be
a me or you.

They reproduce
in different ways.

We hatch from eggs
our mother lays!

Sister Bear
and her brother
grew from eggs
inside their mother.

Some animals are
so very small
they do not come
from eggs at all.

What do these tiny creatures do?

They grow until . . .   they split in two.

So-o-o-o,
if you're ALIVE
and MOVE AROUND,
if you NEED FOOD
and REPRODUCE,
then—
whether you are
mite or moose,
bee, baboon,
or silly goose—
I'm sure that
you can plainly see
an animal IS
what you must be!

THE BEAUTIES OF NATURE ARE ALL AROUND...

As your nature walk guide
I have many duties.
Now let's take a moment
to enjoy nature's beauties.

Feel the hush
of a woodland glade,

the sudden cool
of woodland shade.

After the sunlight
it's hard to see

the moss . . . the vines . . .

the twisty old tree

all reflected
in a woodland pool.

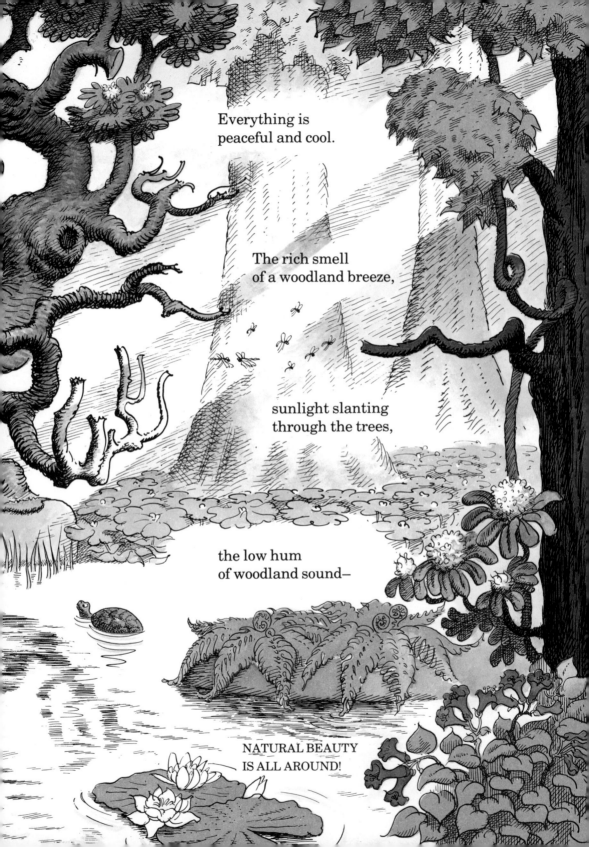

Everything is
peaceful and cool.

The rich smell
of a woodland breeze,

sunlight slanting
through the trees,

the low hum
of woodland sound—

NATURAL BEAUTY
IS ALL AROUND!

MAMMALS

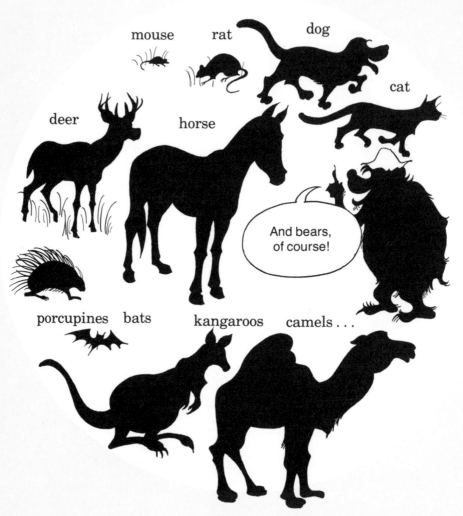

mouse   rat   dog

cat

deer   horse

And bears,
of course!

porcupines   bats   kangaroos   camels . . .

These are all animals
that we call MAMMALS.

Mammals grow
fur or hair.

Some have a lot,
like Great Natural Bear.

Others — just a little,
scattered here and there.

Mammals have their babies live.
That is, MOTHER mammals do.

Some of them
have a lot.

Others — one or two.

Mammals nurse their young.
That is, MOTHER mammals do.

This works very well
when feeding one or two.

But if, like Mother Possum,
you have many mouths to feed,
you are going to have
a busy time indeed.

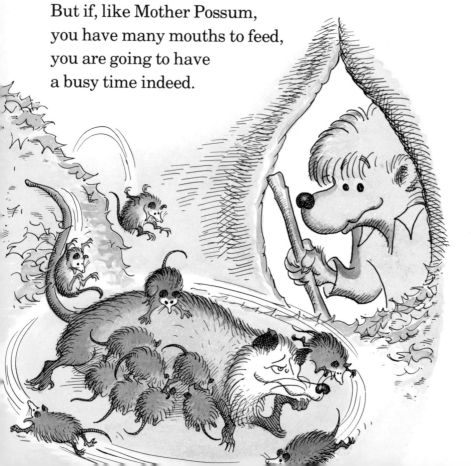

Porpoises and whales—
they are mammals, too.
They nurse their babies
in the sea—
not an easy thing to do.

There are
many strange
and odd-shaped
mammals,
like walruses
and two-humped camels.

But what is really
strange to us
is the funny duck-billed
platypus.
It has a furry body
and furry little legs,
but its feet and bill are duck-like.
And, duck-like, it lays eggs.

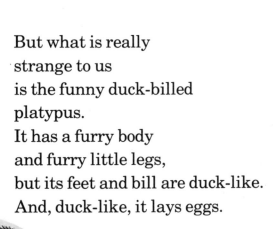

THE BEARS' OFFICIAL BIRD WATCHING STATION

THE BIRDS OFFICIAL BEAR WATCHING STATION

Birds come in many colors and have many different habits.

Robin Redbreast catches worms.

Owls catch mice and rabbits.

Papa Cardinal is very red.

Mama's mostly brown.

The white-breasted nuthatch has dinner upside-down.

The vulture sees
for miles around.

Canada goose
makes a honking sound.

Hermit thrush is very shy.

Hawk is fierce and bold.

Stormy petrel likes the rain.

Junco likes the cold.

Some birds are
very proud.
They say their names
right out loud.

Towhee says, "Towhee! Towhee!"

Chickadee says, "Chickadee-dee-dee!"

Guess who says "Bob White! Bob White!"

If you guessed bobwhite,
you're right!

Oriole's nest
is one of the best.
It's big and strong
and round.

Kildeer builds
no nest at all.
It lays its eggs
on the ground!

On any nature
walk I take,
I always go past
Great Swamp Lake.

Turtles! Lizards!
A water snake!
REPTILES live in
Great Swamp Lake!

If we wait
a little while,
we might even see
a crocodile.

I already
see one, Dad.

GREAT
SWAMP
LAKE

You're standing on him—
AND HE LOOKS MAD!

Reptiles such as
lizard, snake, and crocodile
have been on earth
a long, long while.

Their cousin,
mighty dinosaur,
doesn't live here
any more.

Extinct's the word
for dinosaur.

Dinosaur

Here's the story
of a toad and a frog.
two AMPHIBIANS
from Swampuddle Bog:

One afternoon
a toad and a frog
were napping together
in Swampuddle Bog.

A fine, fat fly
came a-buzzin'
right between
the toad and his cousin.

The toad and the frog
each opened an eye
and thought to themselves,
"A fine, fat fly!

ACTUAL FACTS ABOUT TOADS & FROGS

First, the mother
lays her eggs.

Tads hatch out.

The tads grow legs.

"I'll shoot out my tongue
with a zip and a zap,
have a quick swallow,
and go on with my nap."

Out came the tongues
as quick as a shot
and tied themselves up
in a big sticky knot.

Where was the fly?
The fly was still there,
but the two sticky tongues
were stuck in mid-air!

To untangle them took
the rest of the day
and as for the fly
. . . he got away.

And what do we learn
from that fly that came buzzin'?
Never stick out
your tongue at your cousin!

They grow until   one fine day   they lose their tails   and hop away!

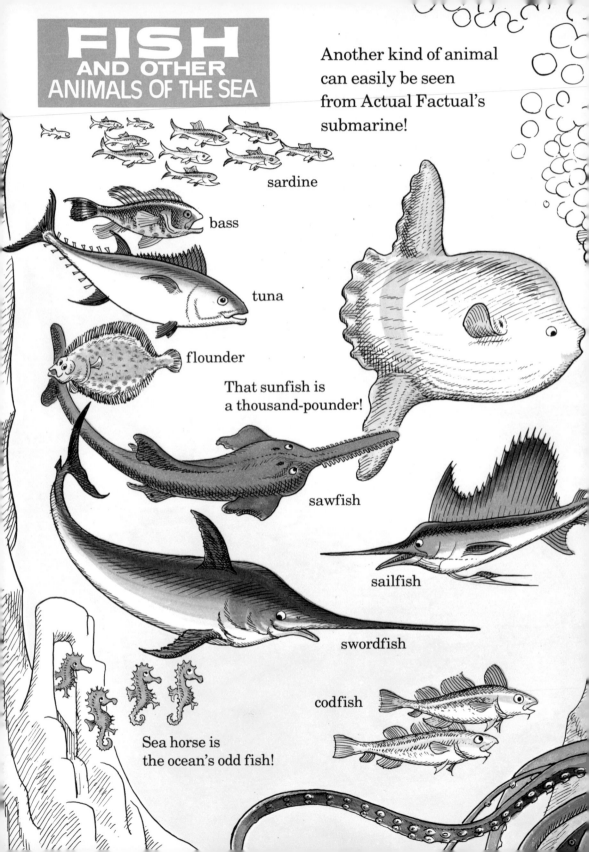

FISH
AND OTHER
ANIMALS OF THE SEA

Another kind of animal can easily be seen from Actual Factual's submarine!

sardine

bass

tuna

flounder

That sunfish is a thousand-pounder!

sawfish

sailfish

swordfish

codfish

Sea horse is the ocean's odd fish!

catfish

hogfish

batfish

dogfish

Dogfish bite
but they can't bark.

The same with
conger eel and shark.

Lobster, crab,
and their relations
form a family
called **crustaceans**.

Octopus
and
giant squid

are similar
but not the same.
Mollusk is their
family name.

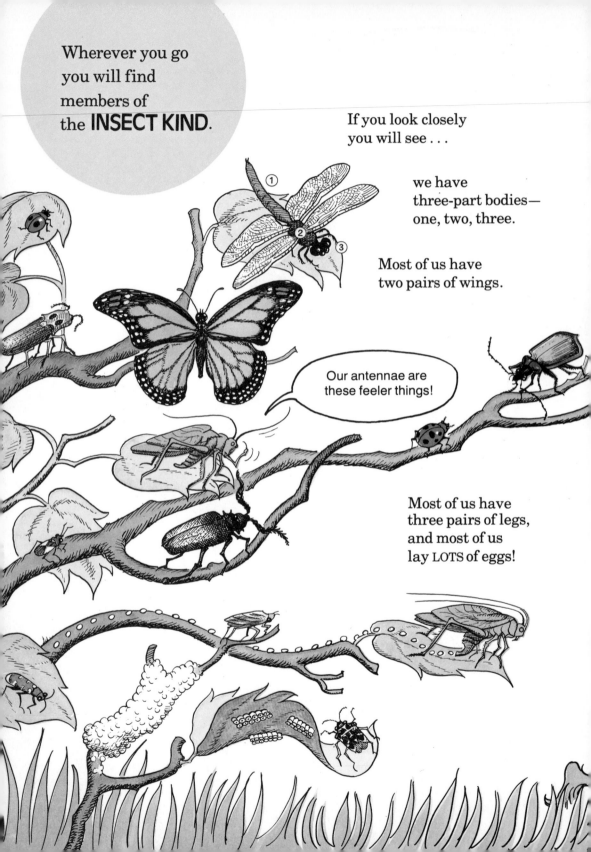

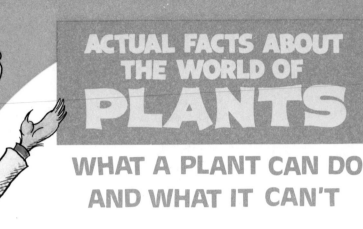

ACTUAL FACTS ABOUT THE WORLD OF PLANTS

WHAT A PLANT CAN DO AND WHAT IT CAN'T

You can visit your friends and watch TV.	A plant can't.
You can jump a puddle and climb a tree.	A plant can't.
You can also read and write.	A plant can't even fly a kite.

But there are things plants CAN do that you and I could NEVER do!

When water rushes through your yard in very rainy weather, all the grass roots underground hold the soil together.

In places where you have no lawn you may find the soil is gone!

Plants are
food for us to eat—

every cabbage,
bean, and beet,
all the rice
and corn
and wheat.

And, in a way,
plants help make meat.

Look at chickens—

THEY feed
on grain and seed.

FARMER BEN'S MARKET

BARBECUED CHICKEN

Have a drumstick?

Yes indeed!

Plants are also
very good
at making different
kinds of wood.

The wood for houses,
boats, and skis

comes from different
kinds of trees.

Even clothes
can come from plants,
like jeans
and cotton underpants.

COTTON
PLANT

Plants help make the air we breathe.
They make a gas called OXYGEN,
the gas we use
when breathing IN.

Plants need a gas
called CO_2,
which they get
from me and you.
WE breathe OUT CO_2.

That's something
we can think about
as we are breathing
in and out.

So, next time
you meet a plant,
remember . . .
what a plant CAN do
is more important
than what it can't.

The biggest, strongest
plant we see
is the kind of plant
we call a tree.

Elm is smooth.

Hickory's rough.

Willow bends.

Oak is tough!

Pine and spruce
are **evergreens**.
They keep their leaves
year round.

The **broad-leafs**
lose theirs in the fall.
You'll find them
lying on the ground.

No matter how many
kinds you name,
in some ways trees
are all the same.

Their roots grow deep
into the ground.
Their trunks of wood
grow thick and round.

Trees are covered
with a skin called bark.
See for yourself.
in a woods or a park.

Flowering plants
are pretty.
Many smell good, too.
But flowers
aren't just pretty—
they have a job to do.
In all such plants,
even WEEDS,
the flower's job
is making seeds.

ESPECIALLY weeds!

Most kinds of plants need water
almost every day.
But not the kind called cactus—
it's built a different way.
Cactus stores up water
in its special stem.
When animals try to get it . . .
OUCH! Too bad for them!

SPLASH!

Algae forms
thick green scum.

Great Natural tried
to walk on some.

The green
one often sees
on the shady side of trees
is moss.

If you study ferns you will find

they don't just grow,

they UNWIND!

When an orange
gets all yucky
because it's very old,
a plant is growing on it.
That yucky plant
is **mold**.

The mushroom is a **fungus**.
It grows from specks
called spores.

WARNING!
NEVER EAT WILD MUSHROOMS—
JUST THOSE
THAT COME FROM STORES

There are some CARNIVOROUS plants
that like to dine on flies and ants.

Like the Venus-flytrap . . .

CRUNCH!
It just had a fly for lunch.

ACTUAL FACTS ABOUT THE EARTH ITSELF

Water helps
to shape the land.

The ocean brings
the shore its sand.

But during storms,
the ocean may
wash some sandy
beach away.

Rivers help
to shape the land.

A river made
Grand Canyon grand!

Freezing water
does its part, too.

Ice can crack
a rock in two.

With the right
amount of rain,
this flat land
we call a **plain**
is a perfect place
for growing grain.

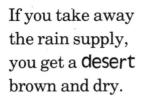

If you take away
the rain supply,
you get a **desert**
brown and dry.

As we cross the land
we can see
how different
its shapes can be.

This high ground
is called a **hill**.

A **mountain**'s
even higher still.

Tall mountains
may be snow-capped.

Others may wear green.

Valley is
the name we give
the low place
in between.

Look Who's Part of the Children's Choice® Family!

Something special for Children's Choice® Book Club members

You can get all these storybook favorites—Puss in Boots, Babar, Curious George, Lyle, George and Martha and The Year at Maple Hill Farm—to hang up on your wall. They're big (17" × 22") and beautiful posters, printed in full color on high quality paper. Best of all, you can get all 6 for just $3.95, including postage and handling.

To order your set of 6 Children's Choice® posters, please send your name, address and $3.95 in check or money order to:

**CHILDREN'S CHOICE®POSTERS
2931 East McCarty St.
P.O. Box 1068
Jefferson City, Mo. 65102**

Please allow 3-6 weeks for delivery. Your posters are mailed in a tube, so they won't be creased at all.

Offer expires August 31. 1981